B & M
POTTERYCRAFTS.

THIRTY STEPS TO CLAY MODELLING.

Brian and Maureen have gone to pot. | Brian Rollins.

Thirty Steps to clay modelling

Introduction.
Part . 1.

The book is split into sections in which all basic pottery skills are described, these skills can be cherry-picked if you wish, they all appear in the sample projects included in the package, all the skills are practiced somewhere in these projects. The sections are not in any particular sequence but each section deals with an overall pottery topic, split into basic skills relating to that topic.

General pottery skills described. Outlines the skills and techniques some or all of which could be used during the making of any pottery model.

Investigate the basic skills of clay preparation. Investigates the initial preparation of the clay and describes how to make the basic shapes and what each could be used to make.

Why thumb pots. Discusses the reasons for using thumb pot techniques in model making and demonstrates how to make successful thumb pots.

Why coil pots? Outlines the reasons for using coil pot techniques and how to produce individual parts and includes the building of a coil pot.

Why slab pots. Gives an outline of the reasons for using these special skills and how they can be applied in clay model making.

Templates and tools discussed. Looks at the use and preparation of templates and the basic tools needed in making clay models.

Part.2.

Clay projects for practice. Contains six projects which lead the student through the basic skills outlined in the 'Thirty Steps' part of the document.

Application and scope.

The information contained in these documents has been developed through practical application of the techniques whilst working with adult students, school children, and special-needs students of all ages.

It has been the intention of **B & M Potterycrafts** to pass on the benefits of the work to **teachers** and **students** who wish to develop their skills in three dimensional art. In preparing the documents I found that the pottery skills needed to produce clay models amounted to **thirty basic skills** and the rest were merely variations or adaptations of these skills.

Six stand-alone projects are included in the '**Section** 2' these demonstrate practical application of the thirty basic skills. When used in a school environment they are intended to cover **Year 1** to **Year6** giving development of all the basic pottery skills throughout junior school. The basic skills introduced can be utilised as **learning objectives,** reinforcing a teacher's learning objectives with individuals through school life.

Projects can be introduced to full classes or smaller groups, and if the instructions are followed several times they will effectively **teach the teacher** or teaching assistant. The whole could be used as a **teach yourself** course.

We have used **air hardening clay** in the demonstrations so that clay modelling can be taught and learned without the use of a kiln, however the information applies equally well to standard school clay followed by the firing process.

In the process of teaching pottery to private groups and in schools **B & M Potterycrafts** have developed literally hundreds of projects based on the techniques outlined and we intend to make them available in the same format as follow-up practical pottery projects which can be used as stand-alone projects or as a library of pottery exercises.

Part 1. Table of contents.

General pottery skills described. 5
- Creation and use of slip. 5
- Crosshatching. 6
- Joining with pressure. 6
- Smooth clay with finger pressure. 7
- Smoothing clay with tools. 7
- Add texture and details. 8
- Mark in the middle. 9
- Cut clay with a knife. 9
- Cut at an angle. 10
- Don't make it too thin. 10
- Why should we weigh clay? 10

Investigate the basic skills of clay preparation. 12
- Roll a smooth ball. 13
- Roll an egg shape. 13
- Make a carrot/cone shape. 14
- Sausage shape. 14
- Make a pancake shape. 15
- Form a point. 17

Why thumb pots? 18
- Create a thumb pot. 18
- Join two thumb pots. 19
- Prepare irregular thumb pots. 20

Why coil pots? 21
- Make and measure a coil. 21
- Make several coils. 22
- Make a loop of clay. 23
- Attach first coil to base. 23
- Build a coil pot. 24

Why slab pots? 26
- Roll clay to a set thickness. 26
- Join slab pot edges. 28

Templates and tools. 29
- Templates. 29
- Work Surfaces. 32

Part. 2.

Practice projects.

General pottery skills described.

Creation and use of slip.

The creation of **slip** is an important part of joining together two pieces of clay

Slip is a mixture of clay and water and can be produced and used in several ways.

It is important to remember that the slip that you use must be produced with the clay that you are using to make any models, when the models are fired the slip will fire to the same colour as the clay, slips produced from other clay will invariably fire a different colour and will show as a seam against the base clay.

The simplest way to produce slip, which is generally only used on small projects, is to use a rough brush to apply water to the parts to be joined together. Both surfaces must be rubbed vigorously with the brush and water until sufficient slip is created on each surface.

Most projects demand slip and a simple way to create it is to add water to a container of wet clay pieces and use a stiff brush or strong table fork to break down the clay and with sufficient energy slip will be produced.

I have found that the way to produce slip in volume is to first dry chunks of clay, of any size and when the clay has dried place it in a container and cover the pieces with water. After a few minutes you will see the clay starting to dissolve as the result of rehydration of the dry clay with the water which is breaking down the crystal lattice of the dry clay. As you can see from the picture in this section the edges of the clay are crumbling and making the water cloudy, this 'slaking down' of the clay will continue until the clay has completely dissolved.

The slip can now be produced by stirring the clay and water into a paste, the consistency depending on what you want to make. For joining pieces of clay together a thick, custard like consistency is practical. Remember you can always stir in a little water to adjust the mixture.

The most practical method to apply the slip is to use a stiff paintbrush which can also be used to further rough up the clay edges.

Crosshatching.

Crosshatching is one of the keys to joining two pieces of clay. It consists of scoring the pieces in the areas to be joined. Use the point of the knife to score the clay, this forms a toothed surface into which slip sinks and helps the edges to be joined to bond together.

As can be seen in the picture scoring of the clay is quite deep and really breaks up the surface to allow the slip to penetrate. Crosshatching is always carried out in what might be called structural assembly of any model, for instance fixing a base to a pencil pot, again demonstrated by the picture, as you can see the rim of the pot and the area of the base to which the sides of the pot will attach are well scored prior to assembly.

Joining with pressure.

The use of **pressure** is essential in successfully joining together two pieces of clay when used in conjunction with crosshatching and slip.

This technique applies equally to surfaces on which slip has been created and the ones to which slip has been applied with a brush.

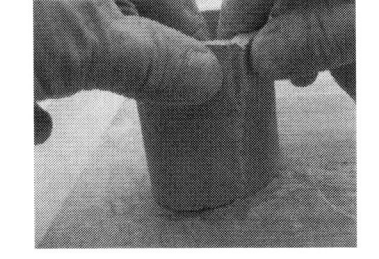

The pressure assists the clay pieces to bond together by squashing one piece into the other and making the joint effectively one piece of clay. Crosshatching or roughing up the clay helps with this by making a larger surface area soft and easier to recombine as one mass of clay.

Applying finger pressure to smooth the joint finishes off the process and strengthens the joint.

Smooth clay with finger pressure.

The smoothing of clay with your fingers or thumbs is used to remove any blemishes left on the clay in the early stages of clay preparation. It is also used in forming and modelling clay.

Finger pressure is also used to remove excess slip from joints and in smoothing the joints themselves making the model appear to be one solid piece rather than several jointed pieces.

The process of smoothing joints actually serves to strengthen the models because pressure round the joint bonds the clay at those points.

This doesn't just apply to coil pots but to all branches of clay work where pieces have to be moulded or joined together and as you will see in another section on smoothing with tools it is sometimes only the first step in the smoothing process.

Smoothing clay with tools.

As I described in the section regarding smoothing clay with the fingers, this is generally only the start of the process, tools are usually employed to produce the finished surface.

The tools can be plastic or metal knives, spatulas, smoothed wooden tools and rubber or metal kidney shaped tools.

Tools can be used to remove clay from the surface but in general the aim isn't to remove clay but to work with the clay when it is still wet to smooth away blemishes, to finish or conceal joints and leave the surface smooth and free from marks.

Check any tools before touching the clay to ensure that the edges are clean and the surfaces are smooth, no point trying to smooth clay with something which will mark the surface. I have mentioned the surface and edges of the tools because these are the areas which will do the work.

As you work clay can stick to the tools and it is important to clean the working surfaces of the tools at regular intervals to stop them marking the clay.

Stroke the smooth surface of the tools across the clay for the best results and try to start each stroke with the edge of the tool off the clay surface as the start of the stroke can mark the clay, even when using a rubber implement, as in every activity practice is the only way to improve.

Add texture and details.

In the previous section we have gone to a great deal of trouble to remove marks from the clay, in this section I will discuss adding texture and finishing touches to our clay models.

This activity is left to the end of most projects because while we are still handling the model it is pointless adding anything which will be obliterated by touching the clay.

The details usually consist of eyes, mouth, toes hair, or drawings on pots.

In the example of the hedgehog in the picture, the eyes and mouth were done using a pointed stick and the spikes and toes were made using the point of a plastic knife.

Parts such as noses, scarves or hats can be added to decorate and complete the model, make sure that they are attached with slip. Material and decorative items can be pressed into the soft clay to produce patterns and textures.

Mark in the middle.

In clay modelling most of the creatures, humanoid or animal have multiples of two legs or arms, to save extra weighing of clay during preparation the strategy is to weigh the clay, measure it against the template as one piece and cut it into two or four equal lengths.

This also serves to add an element of personal judgement, arithmetic and measuring to the exercise.

To ensure an accurate cut into halves or quarters I have used the strategy of first marking the clay where it is to be cut, checking the position of the mark either by judgement or measuring against the template and only when I am satisfied with the position of the mark do I cut the clay.

Cut clay with a knife.

Over the years I have moved away from the implement usually associated with cutting and working clay, the fettling knife.

I have nothing against this type of knife, it as an excellent tool but too dangerous in the hands of young children. I have replaced it by a cheap and versatile plastic knife. Just trim the serrated edge with a pair of scissors and replace this edge by sharpening the trimmed edge on fine sandpaper.

In cutting coils of clay into pieces, such as legs or arms, it is important that the blade is held firmly with the side of the blade at right angles to the clay. Simply press through the clay and slide the blade along the work surface to ensure a clean cut.

When making slab pot models, as in the example in the picture, it is important to keep the cutting edge vertical to the surface to be cut because if the knife is at an angle you will cut under one edge of the slab and over the other edge making it difficult to crosshatch and join cleanly to the next piece. Try to cut in one clean motion, if you stop and restart you will probably leave a jagged edge.

Cut at an angle.

This method of cutting clay to be used as legs or arms for instance, gives you the ability to place the legs or arms in any position on a figure which is generally rounded.

Consider cutting a sausage shape directly across the centre to make two legs to be attached directly to the body. The legs will stick out from the body at right angles to the body, which is fine for a scarecrow or a policeman but net very flexible in positioning.

Cutting the arms or legs at an angle as shown in the picture enables you to position them with much more realism and also with a larger surface to surface contact leading to a stronger joint.

Don't make it too thin.

This paragraph on thin clay is important for several reasons, and the reasons for it become obvious when the clay has dried out and it is brittle and snaps at a touch.

In this condition any handling will break off thin parts such as clay added as fur to a squirrel or thin arms with small contact points added to an octopus.

Make the clay thicker and joints with as large a surface to surface contact as the model allows. Use strategies which allow you to make thin parts, such as drape the octopus over a rock and attach the legs to the body and to the rock.

Why should we weigh clay?

There are several reasons for a potter to weigh clay the main one being repeatability.

By this I mean that if you want to produce models all the same size and dimensions the simplest way is to start with the pieces the same weight.

Over the years I have found that this strategy backed by templates produces models of uniform size.

I developed the strategy soon after we began teaching in schools. As I designed a particular model, for example a Roman Soldier, I assembled the model loosely, that is without slip, and when I was satisfied with the proportions I stripped him down to his component parts and weighed and measured each one.

To simplify the weighing process and to limit the number of pieces we needed to weigh if there were two or more on the model, for example arms, I noted double the weight of one and made two from the extended template. This also adds an element of judgement and measuring skills into the exercise for the students.

If you wish to make several identical **thumb pots** use the strategy of weighing the first one made, then create a suitable template from the model showing diameter and height, your thumb pot can be repeated as many times as you wish. This will also help when you are joining thumb pots together to make a hollow model, the two parts will be identical making it easier to mate the edges.

This also applies to **coil pots**, if you want a straight and even coil pot weigh each piece of clay and as you roll the coils measure them against the template or ruler to keep them identical, don't be tempted to cut bits off- the resultant coil will be thinner than intended. To adjust the length press the ends until you get the correct length.

Investigate the basic skills of clay preparation.

(The starting point).

The reason that I have called this **the *starting point*** is that in all aspects of clay work the clay must first be prepared for use. In most cases this consists of taking the piece of clay to be prepared between the palms of your hands and with sufficient pressure to change the shape roll the clay round and round until a smooth surface is produced. You will find that too much pressure will produce a piece of clay with two conical surfaces. Too little pressure will not provide a smooth surface.

I have twice mentioned **a smooth surface** the reason for this is that in most cases surfaces are smooth to start off the process and pieces, decoration and texture is added to complete the work.

This smooth surface applies to thumb pots but with an extra reason, because in making the thumb pot the clay is stretched and any cracks or creases on the surface will widen and appear as blemishes or weaknesses in the pot.

This also applies to a greater extent in producing a slab pot, the process of rolling the clay flat again produces stress in the clay which will appear as a crack or a weakness and that portion of the slab should not be used.

In the preparation of clay, rolling in the palms of the hands is preferable to using the work surface, though you will learn that there are circumstances when the use of the work surface is both allowed and preferred.

Rolling clay on an absorbent work surface, such as a wooden board, can remove moisture from the clay and cause it to become dry making the clay too hard to work with and causing cracking on the surface. This removal of moisture can however work to your advantage if the batch of clay is too wet and you wish to make it less sticky, rolling it on the board removes moisture, it is a matter of experience and judgement when to roll and when not to roll on the board. In another scenario the table on which the work surface is placed has a plastic, non absorbent, surface which can be used to smooth clay balls without removing moisture. Finally you may have a student with limited use of both hands in which case the work surfaces will help roll the clay using only one hand.

Roll a smooth ball.

(The real starting point.)

This **is** the starting point of most clay activities. The clay must be prepared for subsequent work and manipulation. Before we carry out any of the following activities it is advisable to prepare the clay by forming a smooth ball using the techniques described in the following text.

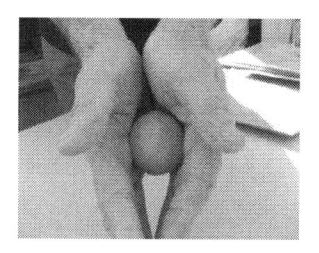

The main reasons for the rolling activity is to remove cracks and creases from the surface of the clay as these will become either blemishes on the surface of the finished object or weaknesses in the structure of models.

To start the rolling process squeeze the piece of clay between the palms of your hands to remove the larger lumps and dents, forming a roughly spherical object. The next stage is to roll the clay firmly, but not too hard, in the palms of the hands to remove the remainder of the surface marks.

Finally, if a smoother surface to the clay is required; a few gentle rolls on the work surface will give a good smooth finish.

Roll an egg shape.

The creation of an egg shape is needed for several reasons. The egg shape can be an animal's body either upright or horizontal a rabbit's head, human torso or head or simply to form eggs in a nest.

Follow the 'roll a ball' instructions to create a smooth ball of clay then place the ball between the palms of the hands and apply gentle rolling pressure across the clay until the desired diameter or length is achieved. I have said diameter or length because the same basic shape could be a long dog's body or a short fat dog's body.

Don't be tempted to roll the shape on the work surface because this will give you a piece with flat ends whereas the use of hands gives a more rounded finish to the ends of the clay.

To finish off the egg-shape use the tips of your fingers and thumbs to mould each end of the shape into the smooth/ rounded shape shown in the picture.

Make a carrot/cone shape.

The creation of a carrot/cone shape involves a special rolling skill. Instead of laying the hand flat on the clay as if to roll a sausage shape the hand is placed at an angle trapping the piece of clay you wish to extend between the hand and the work surface. With sufficient pressure to reform the clay use long rolls across the work surface until the carrot is the form and length required.

Note. With practice this technique can be used to shape a ball of clay or a sausage shape for a cone, a tail or an elephant's trunk.

Sausage shape. (See coil pots).

This is a basic but important skill and is useful in many ways.

It is this technique which allows you to make coil pots, but in its simpler form is used for arms, legs, torso and many other parts of anatomy. You can form anything from pillars

14

to tree trunks or twigs.

The rolling technique begins by rolling the shape between the palms of the hands, making a short, fat sausage shape, this may be sufficient for arms and legs and the length is easily checked against the template.

Continue the rolling on the work surface, use the palms of both hands to roll the clay across the work surface and if the sausage shape is a long one splay the fingers to cover more area. Try to retain a uniform thickness along the length of the sausage.

Choice of the work surface to be used will depend on the results required, remember that an absorbent surface will take moisture from the clay and could result in the clay being too hard to manipulate. If however the clay is wet you could use the action to deliberately take moisture from the clay.

Rolling long sausage shapes or coils is best done on a non absorbent surface such as a classroom work top with a smooth plastic finish.

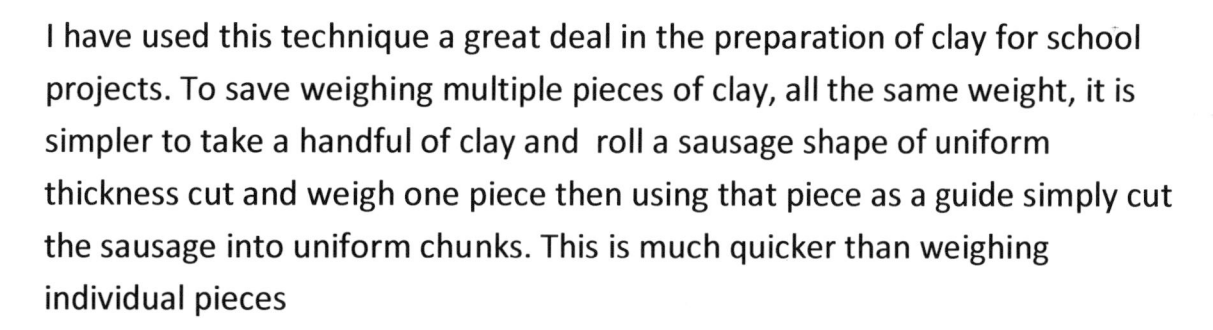

I have used this technique a great deal in the preparation of clay for school projects. To save weighing multiple pieces of clay, all the same weight, it is simpler to take a handful of clay and roll a sausage shape of uniform thickness cut and weigh one piece then using that piece as a guide simply cut the sausage into uniform chunks. This is much quicker than weighing individual pieces

Note. The rolling motion must be quite long as a short roll results in a flat sausage. Each roll across the surface must be long enough to turn the coil/sausage over completely.

Make a pancake shape.

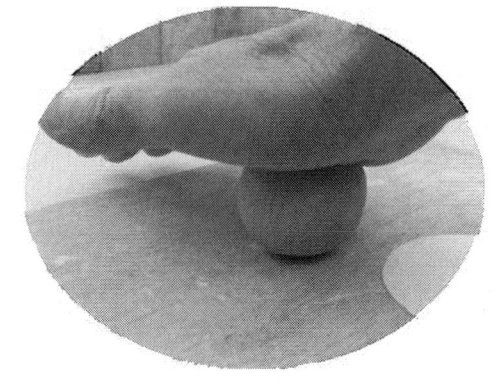

This skill is an alternative method of creating a slab of clay obviating the use of rolling pins. It can be used for smaller slab

pots or for flat rocks or bases on which to stick figures.

Prepare the clay by rolling it into a ball, then squash it as shown in the picture, roughly into the size and shape of the pancake shape that you need. Try to ensure that the thickness is the same across the whole surface of the slab. If it is too thick in places the figure attached will be sloping. If it is too thin in parts the piece will be weak.

If the shape is generally circular then simply roll a ball, if the overall shape is narrower than it is wide first roll the ball into an egg shape, then squash the egg shape with the palm of the hand on the work surface. Flatten the clay a little then check it against the figure and then press it a bit more, repeat this process until the figure fits on the base. Before you attach the figure to the base lift the base and move it to a dry spot on the work surface as the clay can stick to the area on which it was pressed.

There is another application for smaller pancake shapes and that is to make ears.

First roll the clay into a short sausage, mark the middle and then cut it in half, roll the two pieces into two small balls and squash them in the palm of one hand with the thumb of the other hand. The shape shown can be used for models of mice (upright) or pigs (when laid flat).

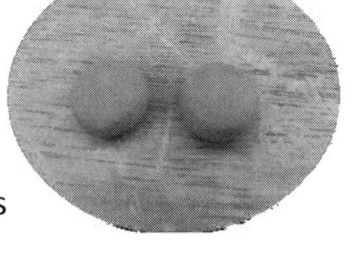

The same process produces semi circular ears for use with elephants, teddy bear or monkey /human models. This time use one piece of clay rolled into a ball, squash it, mark the middle and cut it in half to make the two ears.

Note, a monkey's ears are placed at the side of the head while a teddy bear's ears are almost on top of the head.

Human ears are again at the side of the head but this time placed almost flat.

Form a point.

The formation of a point or cone shaped end on a piece of clay during the process is usually to form a pointed face or nose on an animal model.

Starting with an egg shape hold the piece in one hand and use the tips of the fingers and thumb of the other hand to gently squeeze the clay at one end of the egg shape. This can best be described as arranging the fingers like a drill chuck. Bring pressure to bear evenly around the clay making three shallow finger marks and one mark with the thumb. Turn the clay around a little and repeat the process gradually moving your fingers towards the tip where the clay should be formed into a point.

Finish off the point smoothing the clay by stroking it with the fingers to remove any marks. The example shown in the picture could be the starting point for a hedgehog or a mouse.

Why thumb pots?

Thumb pots are generally used when you are making models demanding a solid piece of clay of over 80 grams in weight, the reason for this is that clay in such volume cannot be fired and remain intact.

During the firing process the clay, even though it may look dry, still contains some moisture and this moisture needs to escape to the surface as steam in the early part of the firing to release any pressure. Smaller pieces of clay can release the pressure but in larger pieces it has nowhere to go so the build up of pressure can blow any weak spots and destroy the model.

The strategy developed to obviate this problem is to either hollow out the model using specialised wire tools or to create **thumb pots.** Single thumb pots or two joined thumb pots are made as the basis of the model. Keeping the wall of an even thickness and less than 1.5 cm thick will enable you to fire the model.

Create a thumb pot.

The first part in creating a thumb pot from a ball of clay is to ensure that the ball is round and smooth as described in the section on making a smooth ball.

The main reasons for this are that if the clay is not smooth before you start to stretch it any cracks will appear as a weakness and the clay will split at those points, to get round this problem check for cracks after each stage of the hollowing and stretching process. Note that if the clay isn't spherical to start you have little chance of finishing with a circular base to the thumb pot.

To start the thumb pot hold the clay in the tips if the fingers of both hands with both thumbs touching the clay, put the thumb nails together until the first knuckles touch each other. Now press your thumbs firmly into the clay leaving two clear impressions like the ones in the picture.

Turn the clay round and put your thumbs back into the hole and press your thumbs into the clay again, making the hole deeper. You can now use the pressure of your thumbs inside the pot against the fingers outside the pot to make the hole deeper and wider, turn the pot round as you gently squeeze the sides of the pot. At this point measure the diameter of your pot against the template on the worksheet, which is the diameter of the pot that you are aiming for. The overall effect can be likened to a half ball or the top of a mushroom.

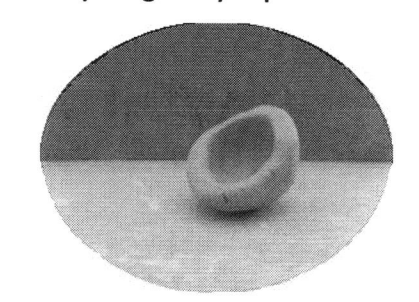

Note. If you wish to make several identical thumb pots I have used the strategy of weighing the first one made, then with reference to a suitable template showing diameter and height your thumb pot can be repeated as many times as you wish.

Join two thumb pots.

Start by making two identical thumb pots using the techniques described in the section on 'make a thumb pot'. Don't forget to weigh the clay and refer to a template.

With the point of the knife crosshatch both of the edges to be joined and create or apply slip to both crosshatched areas.

Hold the half balls in each hand. Bring the two prepared surfaces into contact and press them firmly together with a slight sliding motion across the surfaces to ensure that you get a good bond.

The next part of the process is to seal and hide the joint. First, with the tip of your thumb or finger scrape clay from one half - sphere to the other alternating the strokes, one way then the other to give an even distribution. Use the flat surface of the knife blade like a spatula to further smooth and tidy the join. Finally take the hollow ball of clay in the palms of your hands and treat it like a solid ball by rolling it as you did in preparation, rolling it until it is smooth and free from blemishes. Final smoothing of the bubble of clay can be done on a plastic work surface if a really smooth surface is required.

Note. In the case of a double thumb pot (bubble of clay) it is necessary, for the reasons outlined above to make a hole in the bubble to release pressure during firing.

Prepare irregular thumb pots.

By irregular thumb pots I mean any thumb pot which does not start with a sphere of clay or does not finish as a spherical shape.

The requirement for a hollow shape other than a round or spherical one is that very few figures which you may wish to model are either round or spherical. Most animal or human figures are oval or egg shaped, this is demonstrated in the picture showing the underside view of a hedgehog.

In these cases the trick is to start off by preparing the pieces roughly the same shape as the intended model, so to make a head the starting point would be to prepare two ovoid pieces and make the thumb pots from these pieces. You stand a much better chance of achieving your oval shape using this strategy.

Why coil pots?

Coil pot techniques are normally used to create larger ceramic containers - Ali Baba's jars were probably of coil pot construction. Size is only limited by the length of the potter's arms, the thickness of the pot wall and the size of the kiln at his disposal.

As an exercise in making smaller pots the technique is very versatile and can be used in conjunction with thumb pots and slab pots.

Comparing the technique with thumb pots you can make larger, hollow figures or vessels by building them up one coil at a time and the rolling technique developed for making coils is handy in starting to model parts of figures.

Make and measure a coil.

The rolling technique begins by rolling the shape between the palms of the hands, making a short, fat sausage shape. It is important that the coil is kept to a uniform thickness along the length as it will be difficult to make a pot with coils which vary in thickness.

Having made the short fat sausage continue the rolling on the work surface, use the palms of both hands to roll the clay across the work surface and if the sausage shape is a long one splay the fingers to cover more area and control longer coils..
Complete a few rolls across the work surface, stop and check that the coil is of an even thickness. If the coil is thicker in some parts than in others the next rolling motion should apply pressure to the thicker parts.

With practice coils of a uniform thickness can be produced.

The strategy which I have developed to enable

myself and a class of children to produce coils of uniform thickness is as follows. During the design of the project I make one coil of the thickness and length required and weigh it and note the length. I then include in the worksheet a template of the desired length. Pieces of clay of the same weight, and the coil kept to an even thickness along the length of the coil, and each one is measured against the template then the coils will be identical. As the picture shows coils can be measured against a ruler if this proves easier.

Choice of the work surface to be used will depend on the results required, remember that an absorbent surface will take moisture from the clay and could result in the clay being too hard to manipulate. If however the clay is wet you could use the action to deliberately take moisture from the clay.

I have found that rolling long sausage shapes or coils is best done on a non absorbent surface such as a classroom work top with a smooth plastic finish.

Make several coils.

First roll the clay into a short sausage in the palms of your hands, and then extend the coil by rolling it across a smooth work surface. When you have made your uniform coil you repeat the process to make several coils.

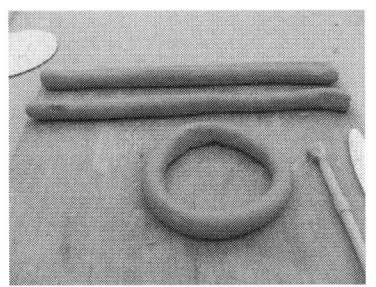

Remember to weigh each piece of clay and as you roll the coils measure them against the template or ruler to keep them identical.

In making larger or taller vessels the temptation is to make all the coils you need and then assemble the coils to form the pot.

This strategy is fine as long as you remember to place the coils not being used immediately in a plastic bag to keep them moist. Some coils take longer to assemble than others and coils left on an absorbent surface will quickly dry and loose malleability and will be difficult to blend together.

Make a loop of clay.

First roll the clay into a short sausage in the palms of your hands, and then extend the coil by rolling it across a smooth work surface. When you have made your uniform coil you can now form the loop.

Gently form the clay into an almost complete circle with the end not quite touching. During the forming process don't force the clay or it will break, just apply gentle pressure with fingers and thumbs to encourage the clay to bend.

Dip your slip brush in the water and rub the water firmly into each end of the loop to form the slip which will bond the ends together.

Hold the ends between fingers and thumbs of both hands press the ends together with a slight sliding motion, one end against the other. Complete the joint by smoothing it with your finger.

Attach first coil to base.

First roll the clay into a short sausage in the palms of your hands, next extend the coil by rolling it across a smooth work surface. When you have made your uniform coil you can form the loop and stick the ends together with slip.

The base should be reasonably thick to give a firm foundation and the same diameter as the loop.

With water and the slip brush create slip round the base where the coil is to be attached and also on the coil where it will   touch the base. Firmly press the coil onto the base using pressure from fingers and thumbs.

Holding the coil in position on the base with the fingers and thumb of one hand press clay from the coil into the base with the tip of the thumb of the other hand. Gradually turn the pot round pressing clay from coil to base until you return to the start point, the first coil is now firmly fixed to the base.

Note. The coil could be attached inside as well as outside however if you just do the outside you can clearly see the assembly technique inside the pot.

Build a coil pot.

When making a cylinder the easiest way is to use pre weighed clay for the coils and a template to standardise the length of each coil. If you roll each coil with an even thickness you will make all the coils the same size making the pot easier to build.

The base should be reasonably thick to give a firm foundation with the same circumference as the coils.

Make the base and the first coil and create or apply slip to both the base and the coil and press the coil firmly onto the base. Holding the coil in position on the base with the fingers and thumb of one hand press clay from the coil into the base with the tip of the thumb of the other hand. Gradually turn the pot round and press clay from coil to base until you return to the start point, the first coil is now firmly fixed to the base.

Progressively add coils until you reach the depth of pot required. One point to remember is to place the joint of each coil in a different position on the pot because a line of joints will give a weak spot through the pot.

When you have made the pot to the depth required smooth the outside surface with fingers and thumbs to remove the worst blemishes and finish off the smoothing using the surface of the plastic knife flat against the pot.

Stroke the smooth surface of the tools across the clay for the best results and try to start each stroke off the clay surface as the start of the stroke can mark the clay, even a rubber kidney. **Note.** The coils can be attached and smoothed inside as well as outside however if you just do the outside you can clearly see the assembly technique inside the pot.

Why slab pots?

Slab pots are made from slabs of clay cut to the required size and fixed together with crosshatching and slip, the size again only limited by the thickness of the clay used to build the pot combined with the size of the kiln.

In working with schools I have developed more slab pot projects than any of the other disciplines which is an indication of the flexibility and versatility possible using these techniques.

I have developed projects for containers and houses, numerous decorated plaques, three layer figures and animals, even a Viking long ship.

Roll clay to a set thickness.

The term **slab pot** refers to clay which has been prepared and rolled flat with a rolling pin or flattened by squashing and pressing. The former technique, when coupled with flat sticks of a given thickness, provides the most repeatable and standard results.

Start by rolling a piece of clay into a round smooth ball in the palms of your hands carefully removing any cracks or creases with finger pressure as they will become weak spots as soon as the clay is rolled and stretched.

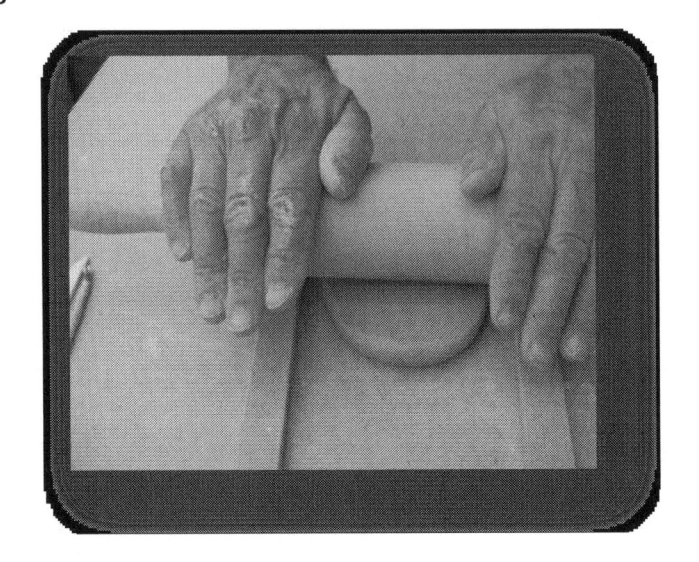

When the clay is smooth it is patted flat before starting to use the rolling pin, you make it flat first because it is difficult to start the rolling process from the top of a ball. At this stage check again for any cracks appearing round the edges of the flattened ball due to stressing the clay by flattening it, if any cracks appear repair them with pressure from your fingers. Repeat these checks and repairs throughout the process.

As you can see in the picture the hands are placed on top of the rolling pin not on the handles, this way you can exert more downward pressure through the clay to the work surface. Use of sticks of a set thickness allows you to produce slabs of clay to a known and uniform thickness every time simply by ensuring that the rolling only stops when the rolling pin is touching the top of both sticks. **Note.** Always keep the ends of the rolling pin over the sticks.

Several times during the rolling it is advisable to peel and lift the clay from the work surface because it sticks to the surface and constant rolling won't make it thinner, lifting and replacing the clay on the work surface allows you to start again and makes the stretching of the clay easier, it can be compared to Granny spreading flour on her work surface when rolling pastry, it stops it sticking to the work surface and to the rolling pin. When the board becomes very wet it may be better to find a dry spot, turn the board over or even use a replacement board.

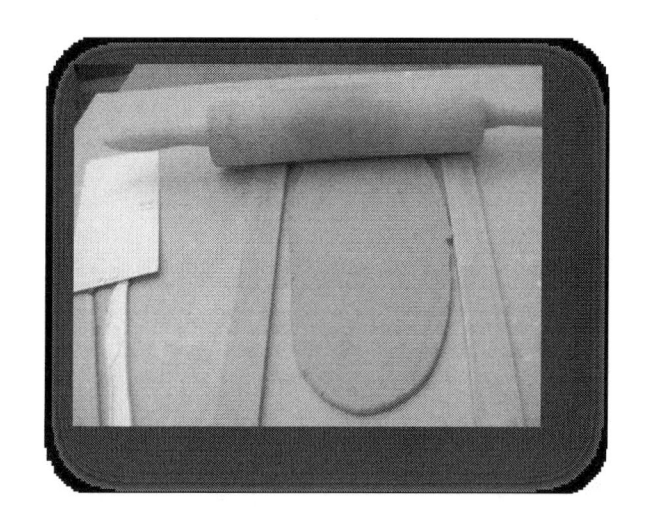

The second picture in this section demonstrates the ways in which you can minimise the amount of clay needed for each job, I have said that we should produce a round, smooth ball of clay, a ball rolled flat in one direction produces the result shown which is fine for longer slabs of clay but needs a different strategy to produce a circular slab.

In order to produce a larger slab it is necessary to roll the clay in one direction for a while, turn it round through ninety degrees and roll it some more. Repeat the rolling and turning until you achieve the desired result.

In order to produce a particular shape of slab the best strategy is to start with the general shape which you want to produce and you stand a good chance of finishing with the desired shape. This strategy also reduces the weight of clay you need to start the process, if you need a square slab, start with a square block, if you need a long strip start with a flattened sausage shape.

Join slab pot edges.

The techniques employed in jointing slab pot edges are the same ones used in all clay work consisting of cross hatching the areas to be joined and creating or applying slip and pressing these areas together as summarised below.

Crosshatching is one of the keys to joining two pieces of clay. It consists of scoring the pieces in the areas to be joined. Use the point of the knife to score clay in the pattern shown in the picture. Apply the slip liberally to both areas to be joined then press the parts together with a slight sliding motion.

The joint can be finished with pressure from fingers and the flat edge plastic knife or spatula.

Templates and tools.

Templates.

The use of templates ensures repeatability, and coupled with weighing each clay part serves to avoid reinventing the wheel every time you decide to make a particular figure.

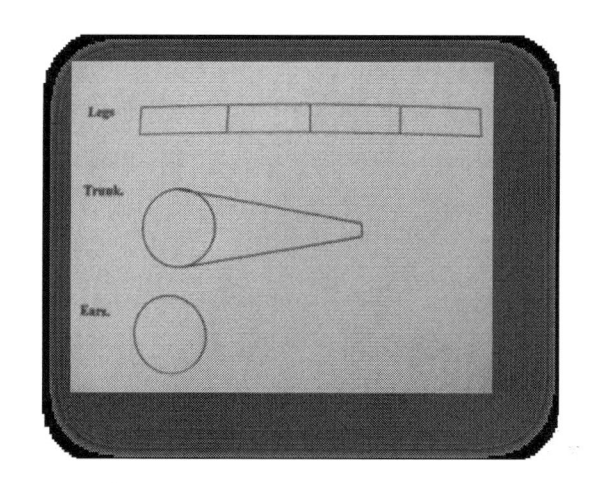

This first example of templates shows the ones I used to make a model elephant. They are produced to scale using rulers and drawing techniques available in the word processing package used to produce the documents.

Each one is marked with the part you need to make (and the weight of the clay for that part) and if the model has more than one of the part, say legs, the template allows you to make one long coil and cut it to lengths suitable to the scale of the model. The circle would likewise be cut in half to make two ears.

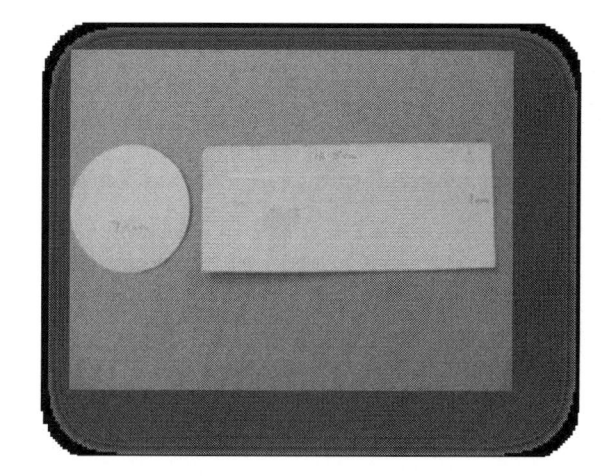

The second example shows the two simple card templates needed to make a pencil pot using slab pot techniques. The circle produces the base and the rectangle, when formed into a tube shape and the edges joined by crosshatch and slip, forms the body of the pot ready to be slipped onto the base.

Using this strategy coupled with weighing clay limits the amount of clay needed to make the pot and the amount wasted or set aside for recycling.

Tools.

In this section I will outline which tools are needed to perform the tasks and skills described in the book.

All the tools can be bought in craft or hobby shops or you can produce cheap alternatives which are just as good and in some cases better and more suitable for use in schools.

Modelling tools shown in this section are the simple tools needed for sculpting small models, most thumb pots and most coil pots.

The paint brush is chosen for its stiff bristles which allow you to rough up the clay to help with cross hatching or obviate the need for cross hatching in some circumstances.

Plastic knives with the serrated edges trimmed using scissors and sharpened on sand paper are a cheap alternative to a potter's fettling knife and more suitable for use by young children. They are used primarily for cutting lengths of clay but can be used as a spatula to smooth joints between pieces of clay.

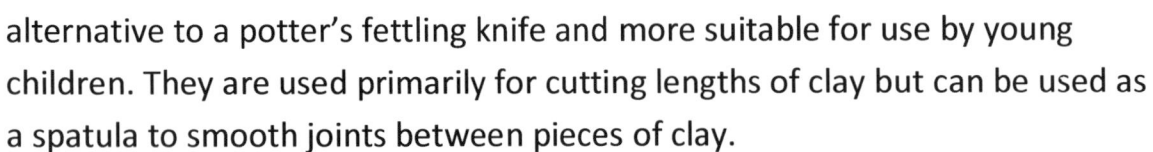

Pencils or pointed sticks, shown in the picture, are used for adding details such as eyes or hair to models or drawing patterns and designs on pots of all descriptions. The pointed stick shown was made from 3mm thick skewers used in cooking Kebabs. Cut the skewer to the length you need, I got three from one skewer, sharpen one end and round off the other end using sand paper.

Further examples of tools used for smoothing clay surfaces or joints are shown in the separate pictures. Because of their shape they are called 'kidneys', the dark one is made of spring steel and is called a metal kidney while the red one is made from a hard, flexible rubber and is called a rubber kidney.

Both are very effective and the rubber one is held with the thumb on the flat working surface and the fingers loosely holding the rounded top of the kidney. In the case of the metal kidney which is flat on both sides either working surface can be used.

The only other tools for consideration in this document are the ones used in the preparation of clay for slab pots. These are shown in the picture and consist of a rolling pin and a pair of flat sticks. Clay is flattened by the rolling pin to a controlled thickness by placing it between the sticks and rolling it until the rolling pin reaches the sticks when it will be the same thickness as the sticks, in this case 6mm as noted on each stick.

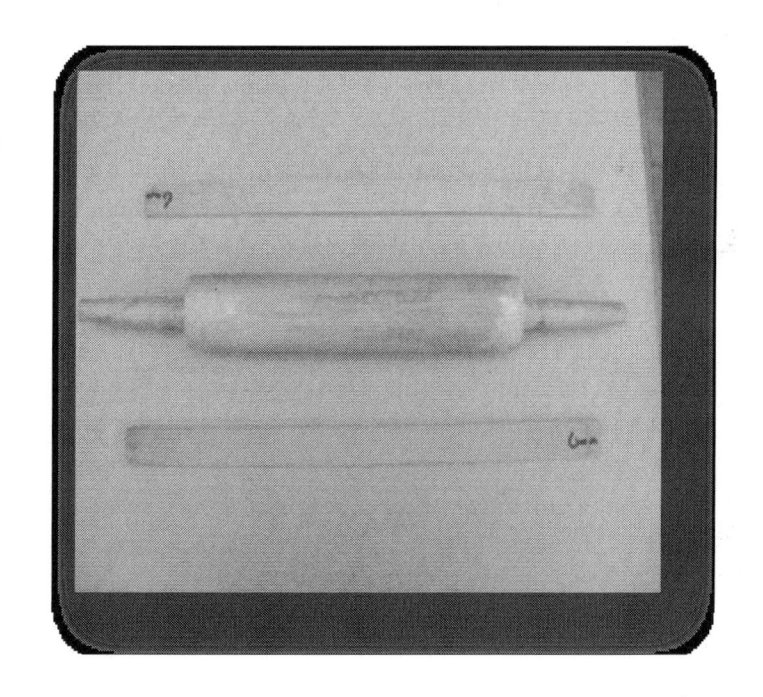

Rolling pins are available at most craft suppliers, hardware stores or super markets, make sure that the rolling pin you choose is free from cracks or blemishes which will mark the clay. Remember that a smooth rolling pin will give you a smooth slab of clay with which to work. The rolling pin shown has handles which are not absolutely necessary as the rolling is done with the hands on the body of the pin to give more downward pressure through the clay.

The sticks shown are 40 cm long, 24 mm wide and 6mm thick. This material is available from DIY shops in two metre lengths and can be purchased in various thicknesses in 3mm steps up to 12mm which should cover any slab pot requirements, I found that 24 mm width was the most practical width to use.

Work Surfaces.

The work surfaces shown in this section and throughout the book are available from craft suppliers or wood suppliers.

The dimensions are 30 x 20 cm 3 ply for the personal work surface and 40 x 40 cm chipboard for the rolling surfaces.

These work surfaces help to protect classroom worktops.

Thirty Steps to clay modelling.

Part 2. Contents.

Practical projects.

Make a mouse.

Make an upright hedgehog.

Thumb pot elephant.

Double thumb pot pig.

Coil pot container.

Slab pencil pot.

Make a clay mouse.

Hand modelling techniques.

B & M Potterycrafts.

B & M Potterycrafts.

Sequence.

Make a Mouse. 36

   Roll a ball. 36
   Make an egg shape. 36
   Make a pointed nose. 37
   Make eyes. 37
   Make and fit ears. 37
   .Make and fit the tail. 38
   Nose, mouth and whiskers. 38
   Make a mouse worksheet. 39

Make a Mouse.

Roll a ball.

Roll the clay between the palms of your hands, exerting sufficient force to remove any lumps or bumps. Don't be tempted to take the easy route to smooth the clay by rolling it on the wooden work surface as this removes moisture from the clay and could make it too hard for modelling. Any creases or cracks can be smoothed using the fingers. Continue to roll the clay until the surface is smooth and the clay is the desired shape i.e. a ball shape.

Make an egg shape.

Take the clay ball between the palms of your hands and roll it into an egg shape. Roll the clay backwards and forwards across your palms exerting sufficient pressure to form the egg shape. The best way is to roll the clay a few times, check the shape then roll it a bit more, keep rolling and checking until you get the shape that you need. Complete the shape by rounding off the ends of the egg with pressure from your fingers and thumbs.

Make a pointed nose.

The next part of the exercise is to form one end of the egg shape into a cone shape, the modelling is done by using the fingers and thumb of one hand while holding the egg shape firmly in the other hand. Press and squeeze the clay between the fingers and thumb, turn the clay round a bit and press and squeeze again, repeat this until the cone shape shown in the picture is formed. Give the nose a smooth surface by sliding your fingers across the surface until it is smooth.

Make eyes.

Use the pointed stick to make two holes to represent the eyes of the mouse.

Make and fit ears.

First make two slots to place the ears into by pressing the blunt end of the plastic knife into the clay as shown in the picture.

Next roll the clay into a ball and then into a short sausage shape, cut the sausage shape in half and roll the pieces into two balls. Squash these small balls in the palm of your hand with the thumb forming two discs. Dip the brush in water and rub the water firmly into the two slots to form **slip,** again with water on the brush make slip on one edge of each ear. Press the ears firmly into the hole, slip to slip.

The creation of **slip** is an important part of joining together two pieces of clay. The water from the brush is rubbed firmly into the clay surface until it turns light grey

The use of **pressure** is essential in successfully joining two pieces of clay when used in conjunction with crosshatching and slip.

Make and fit the tail.

Roll the clay into a smooth ball and then use the palms of your hands to roll a sausage shape to form the tail, use the template on the worksheet to check the correct length. With the brush and water make a line of slip on the mouse's back and also along the length of the tail. Press one end of the tail onto the mouse and stick the tail along his back as shown in the pictures.

Nose, mouth and whiskers.

Take a small piece of clay to make the tip of the mouse's nose, roll it into a ball, and by making slip on the ball and on the tip of the nose area fix the tip to the face.

Use the pointed stick to give the mouse a 'smiley mouth' and whiskers on each side of his face.

B & M Potterycrafts.

Make a mouse worksheet.

Clay.

Body. 80 grams.

Tail.   2 grams.

Nose. Small ball.

Ears. 2grams.

Tail template.   [   ]   3cms.

It is important to copy the worksheet to scale, use the dimensions shown to ensure your model is made to scale.

Make an upright hedgehog.

Hand modelling techniques.

Brian Rollins.

40

B & M Potterycrafts.
Contents and sequence.

Upright Hedgehog. 42

Roll a ball. 42

Make an egg shape. 42

Make the head. 43

Attach the head to the body. 43

Model head to body. 44

Make and fit the arms. 44

Nose. 45

Eyes and ears. 45

Spikes. 45

Upright Hedgehog Worksheet. 46

Upright Hedgehog.

Roll a ball.
Roll the clay between the palms of your hands, exerting sufficient force to remove any lumps or bumps. Don't be tempted to take the easy route to smooth the clay by rolling it on the wooden work surface as this removes moisture from the clay and could make it too hard for modelling. Any creases or cracks can be smoothed using the fingers. Continue to roll the clay until the surface is smooth and the clay is the desired shape i.e. a ball shape.

Make an egg shape.
Take the clay ball between the palms of your hands and roll it into an egg shape. Roll the clay backwards and forwards across your palms exerting sufficient pressure to form the egg shape. The best way is to roll the clay a few times, check the shape then roll it a bit more, keep rolling and checking until you get the shape that you need. Complete the shape by rounding off the ends of the egg with your fingers.

Make the head.

To form the head roll the clay into a smooth ball then into an egg shape, then with fingers and thumb form one end of the egg shape into a point to the shape shown on the picture.

Attach the head to the body.

To attach the head to the body we need to make **crosshatch** marks and create **slip**. With the point of the plastic knife score **'#'** on the top of the body and on the head where it is to be joined to the body. Dip the brush in water and firmly rub the brush and water across the '#' marks, the area will turn white and this material is **slip**. Finally **press** the head and body firmly together.

The creation of **slip** is an important part of joining together two pieces of clay. The water from the brush is rubbed firmly into the clay surface until it turns light grey

Crosshatching is one of the keys to joining two pieces of clay. It consists of the scoring the pieces in the areas to be joined. Use the point of the knife to mark clay.

The use of **pressure** is essential in successfully joining two pieces of clay when used in conjunction with crosshatching and slip.

Model head to body.

With your finger or thumb smooth clay from the head onto the body, this is only from one side of the head to the other side, not under the chin.

Make and fit the feet.

Roll the clay into a smooth ball and then roll it backwards and forwards to form a jellybean shape to the length shown on the worksheet, cut this in half to make the feet. Use the brush and water to form slip in two patches where the feet are to fit, make slip on the feet where they have been cut and press the feet into place.

Make and fit the arms.

Roll the clay into a sausage to the length shown in the worksheet, cut the sausage in half to make two arms.

Create slip on the body where the arms are to fit and on the arms where they will touch the body. Press the arms firmly into place and smooth the tops to form them to the body as shoulders.

Make the nose.

Take a small piece of clay and roll it into a ball, dip the brush in water and rub the water on the top of the pointed end of the head and on one side of the small ball press the nose firmly onto the face.

Eyes and ears.

The eyes are easily made with the pointed end of the stick, push the point into the clay in the positions shown on the worksheet.

Use the pointed end of the stick again to make curly 'c's to represent the ears.

Spikes.

Hold your knife like a pencil and carefully draw short lines from the head down to the tail end of the hedgehog, start between the ears and cover the back and sides of the model.

Hedgehogs don't have spikes on their stomachs so leave the front smooth.

B & M Potterycrafts.

Upright Hedgehog Worksheet.

Clay.

Body. 80grams.

Head. 15grams.

Arms. 10grams. ⬜ 7 cms.

Feet. 4grams. ⬜

Nose. Small piece.

It is important to copy the worksheet to scale, use the dimensions shown to ensure your model is made to scale.

Make a thumb pot elephant.

Thumb pot techniques.

B & M Potterycrafts.

B & M pottery rafts.

Contents/ Sequence.

Single thumb-pot elephant. **49**
    Roll a ball. 49
    Create a thumb pot. 49
    Make and fit head to body. 50
    Make and fit the legs. 51
    Make and fit the arms. 52
    Make and fit the trunk. 52
    Make and fit the ears. 53
    Make and fit the tail. 54
    Decoration and details. 54
    The end. 55
    Worksheet. 56

Single thumb pot elephant.

Roll a ball.

Roll the clay between the palms of your hands, exerting sufficient force to remove any lumps or bumps. Don't be tempted to take the easy route to smooth the clay by rolling it on the wooden work surface as this removes moisture from the clay and could make it too hard for modelling. Any creases or cracks can be smoothed using the fingers. Continue to roll the clay until the surface is smooth and the clay is the desired shape i.e. a ball shape.

Create a thumb pot.

The first part in creating a thumb pot from a ball of clay is to ensure that the ball is round and smooth as described in the previous passage.

The main reasons for this are that if the clay is not smooth before you start to stretch it any cracks will appear as a weakness and the clay will split at those points and if it isn't round to start you have little chance of finishing with a circular base to the thumb pot.

To start the thumb pot hold the clay in the tips if the fingers of both hands with both thumbs touching the clay, put the thumb nails together until the first knuckles touch each other. Now press your thumbs firmly into the clay leaving two clear impressions like the ones in the picture.

Turn the clay round and put your thumbs back into the hole and press your thumbs into the clay again, making the hole deeper.

You can now use the pressure of your thumbs inside the pot against the fingers outside the pot to make the hole deeper and wider, turn the pot round as you gently squeeze the sides of the pot. At this point measure the diameter of your pot against the template on the worksheet. That is the diameter of the pot that you are aiming for. To check that the depth of the pot is correct compare the shape with the rabbit's body on the worksheet, is it in proportion to the diameter?

The overall effect can be likened to a half ball or the top of a mushroom.

Make and fit head to body.
To make the head the clay must first be rolled into a ball, as described in the first paragraph. Take the clay between the palms of your hands and roll it until it is smooth.

Joining the head to the body calls for each piece to be scored in the fashion shown, noughts and crosses marks are scratched into the clay with the point of the knife, this scoring is called **cross hatching** and is used in cunjunction with **slip** to securely join two pieces of clay.

Crosshatching is one of the keys to joining two pieces of clay. It consists of the scoring the pieces in the areas to be joined. Use the point of the knife to score clay.

The creation of **slip** is an important part of joining together two pieces of clay. The water from the brush is rubbed firmly into the clay surface until it turns light grey this is the slip and act as our glue.

The use of **pressure** is essential in successfully joining two pieces of clay when used in conjunction with crosshatching and slip.

Apply slip with the brush to both areas of crosshatching.

With the fingers inside the body supporting the crosshatched area firmly press the head and the body together, slip to slip.

You can check that you have made a good joint by lifting the model from the work surface holding the head between finger and thumb.

Make and fit the legs.
To make the legs start by rolling the clay into a smooth ball and then into a short sausage. Check the length of the sausage by comparing it with the template on the

worksheet. Mark the clay across the centre, not directly across the centre, but at an angle as shown in the picture. Once you are satisfied that the mark is across the centre cut the clay cleanly in half.

Fit the back legs first by crosshatching in the areas shown, add water to the brush and make slip in these areas and press the legs firmly into place.

Make and fit the arms.

The front legs or arms are then made by the same process, this time crosshatching the body at each side close to the head, rotate the each arm to find the best angle to attach it, when you are satisfied with the position create slip on the crosshatch marks and press the front legs firmly into position. Be sure to leave sufficient room to fit the trunk.

Make and fit the trunk.

The creation of a carrot/cone shape involves a special rolling skill. Instead of laying the hand flat on the clay as if to roll a sausage shape the hand is placed at an angle trapping the piece of clay you wish to extend between the hand and the work surface. With sufficient pressure to reform the clay use long rolls across the work surface until the carrot is the form and length required.

To complete the trunk shape you take the thick end of the carrot shape betweem the thumb and the first two fingers and squash it to form a spoon shape and place it in position at the front of the head.

To fit the trunk to the body crosshatch the inside surface of the spoon and the front of the head, create slip in these areas and press the trunk onto the front of the head.

Complete the fitting of the trunk by drawing the clay from the trunk onto the head all around the spoon shape with the fingers smoothing and hiding the joint as shown in the picture.

Make and fit the ears.
The ears are started by rolling the clay into a smooth ball and squashing the ball between the palms of your hands until you form a disc the same diameter as the template.

Mark the disc across the centre and then cut the disc in half to make two ears.

The ears are fitted to the back and side of the head as shown in the picture. Create slip in the areas where the ears are to be attached and in order to make the joint stronger the lower end of the ears are fixed to the elephant's back as well as to the head. Finally press the ears firmly into place.

Make and fit the tail.

Roll the clay into a short sausage and then make slip along the length of the tail and also at the back of the elephant and finally pres the tail onto the body positioned as shown in the picture above.

Decoration and details.

If you are not sure where to position the details such as eyes you can refer to the picture in this section.

Complete the elephant using the pointed stick to make eyes and nostrils simply push the pointed end of the stick into the clay to make the marks.

Use the rounded end of the stick for toenails pressing the edge five times into the top edge of each foot.

Use and the edge of the knife for the wrinkles down the trunk pressing it into the clay to make the marks.

The end.

Worksheet. Single thumb pot elephant.

Clay.

Head. 40 grams.

Arms and Legs. 25 grams.

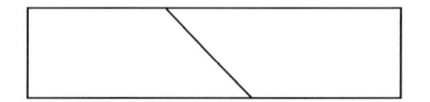

Trunk. 15 grams.

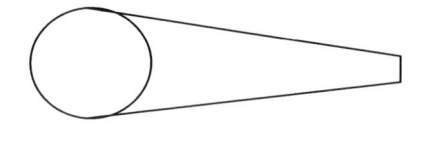

Tail 1 gram.

Ears. 15 grams

Body. 100 grams.

Template. Body.

6 cms.

It is important to copy the worksheet to scale to ensure that your model's proportions are correct

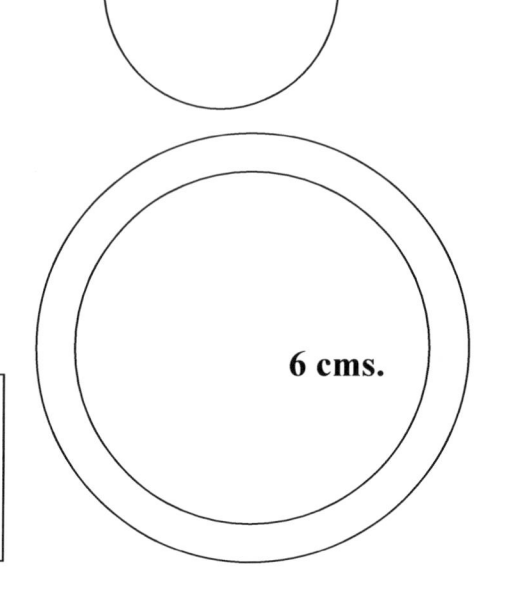

Thumb pot pig.

Join two thumb pots.

Brian Rollins.

B & M Potterycrafts.

Contents/Sequence.

Double thumb pot pig. 59
    Create a single thumb pot. 59
    Make a second thumb pot. 60
    Join two thumb pots. 60
    Make the snout. 61
    Make eyes, mouth and nose and fit the ears. 61
    Make and fit the legs. 61
    Make and fit the tail. 62
    Make the base and fit the pig. 62
    Thumb pot pig worksheet. 64

Double thumb pot pig.

Create a single thumb pot.

The first part in creating a thumb pot from a ball of clay is to ensure that the ball is round and smooth.

Roll the clay between the palms of your hands, exerting sufficient force to remove any lumps or bumps. Don't be tempted to take the easy route to smooth the clay by rolling it on the wooden work surface as this removes moisture from the clay and could make it too hard for modelling . Any creases or cracks can be smoothed using the fingers. Continue to roll the clay until the surface is smooth and the clay is the desired shape i.e. a ball shape.

The main reasons for this are that if the clay is not smooth before you start to stretch it any cracks will appear as a weakness and the clay will split at those points, to get round this problem is to check for cracks after each stage of the hollowing and stretching process. If the clay isn't spherical to start you have little chance of finishing with a circular base to the thumb pot.

To start the thumb pot hold the clay in the tips if the fingers of both hands with both thumbs touching the clay, put the thumb nails together until the first knuckles touch each other. Now press your thumbs firmly into the clay leaving two clear impressions like the ones in the picture.

Turn the clay round and put your thumbs back into the hole and press your thumbs into the clay again, making the hole deeper. You can now use the pressure of your thumbs inside the pot against the fingers outside the pot to make the hole deeper and wider, turn the pot round as you gently squeeze the sides of the pot. At this point measure the diameter of your pot against the template on the worksheet, which is the diameter of the pot that you are aiming for. The overall effect can be likened to a half ball or the top of a mushroom.

Make a second thumb pot.
Repeat the previous section to make a second, identical thumb pot.

Join two thumb pots.
With the point of the knife **crosshatch** both of the edges to be joined and create **slip** on both surfaces by rubbing the brush loaded with water across the crosshatch marks.

The creation of **slip** is an important part of joining together two pieces of clay. The water from the brush is rubbed firmly into the clay surface until it turns light grey

Crosshatching is one of the keys to joining two pieces of clay. It consists of the scoring the pieces in the areas to be joined. Use the point of the knife to mark clay.

The use of **pressure** is essential in successfully joining two pieces of clay when used in conjunction with crosshatching and slip.

Hold the half-balls, one in each hand, bring the two prepared surfaces into contact and press them firmly together with a slight sliding motion across the surfaces to ensure that you get a good bond.

The next part of the process is to seal and hide the joint. First, with the tip of your thumb or finger scrape clay from one half - sphere to the other alternating the strokes, one way then the other to give an even distribution. Use the flat surface of the knife blade like a spatula to further smooth and tidy the join. Finally take the hollow ball of clay in the palms of your hands and treat it like a solid ball by rolling it as you did in preparation, rolling it until it is smooth and free from blemishes. Final smoothing of the bubble of clay can be done on a plastic work surface if a really smooth surface is required.

Make The Snout.

Making the snout begins with rolling the clay into a smooth ball and then squashing it slightly with your thumb on the work surface, creating a thick disc. Crosshatch one side of the disc and a similar sized area on the thumb pot. Create slip by rubbing the brush loaded with water across the crosshatched surface, you will notice that the surface goes slightly lighter in colour.

Support the bubble of clay in the palm of one hand and carefully press the snout onto the body.

Make eyes, mouth and nose and fit the ears.

Use the pointed stick to make the pig's eyes and nostrils and cut the mouth into the snout using the edge of the knife.

To make the ears first roll the clay into a short sausage, mark the middle and then cut it in half, roll the two pieces into two small balls and squash them in the palm of one hand with the thumb of the other hand.

To fit the ears crosshatch two patches immediately above the eyes and also crosshatch the two discs where the ears will attach to the pig.

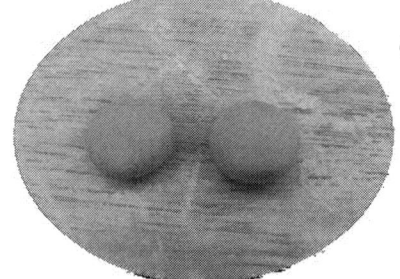

Create slip in the crosshatch marks on the body and on the ears and press the ears firmly into place. Complete this activity by smoothing the ears onto the head.

Make and fit the legs.

Take the clay in the palms of your hands and roll it onto a sausage shape, try to maintain a uniform thickness along the length of the sausage shape. Check the length against the template and finally tidy up the ends by tapping the sausage shape on the work surface.

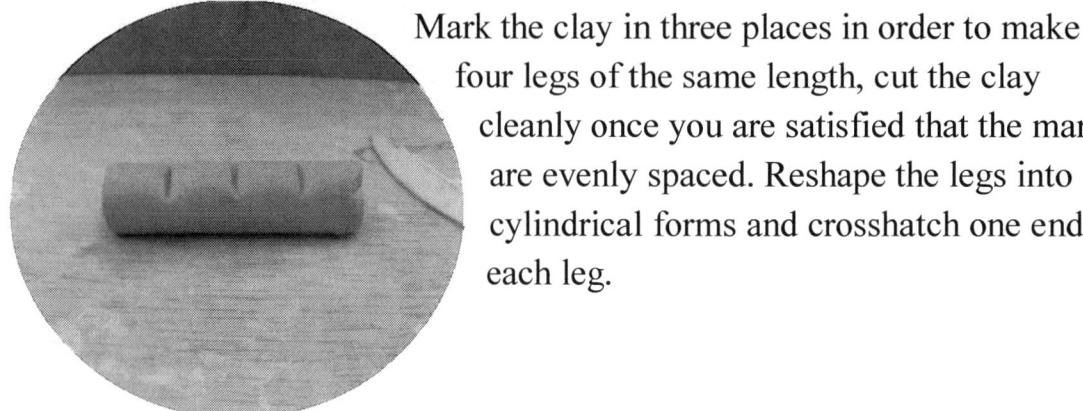

Mark the clay in three places in order to make four legs of the same length, cut the clay cleanly once you are satisfied that the marks are evenly spaced. Reshape the legs into cylindrical forms and crosshatch one end of each leg.

Crosshatch the underside of the pig's body in the places where the legs are to be fitted. The positioning is shown on the picture.

Create slip on the body and on each leg by rubbing water into the crosshatch marks with the brush.

In order to prevent distortion in the ball of clay support the body in the palm of one hand while you press and twist the legs into poition.

Make and fit the tail.

Roll thclay ito a short, thin sausage shape to form the tial, create a patch of slip on the spot where the tail is to attach and also along the length of the tail. Press one end of the tail into the body and twist the tial round between thumb and finger and press the curly tail into the slip on the body.

Make the base and fit the pig.

Prepare the clay by rolling it into a ball, then squash it as shown in the picture, roughly into the size and shape of the pancake shape which you need. Try to

62

ensure that the thickness is the same across the whole surface of the slab. If it is too thick in places the figure attached will be sloping. If it is too thin in parts the piece will be weak.

Mark the base where the feet touch and make crosshatch areas in thesepositions.

Crosshatch the ends of the legs and make slip on the base and on the legs. Place the ends of the legs onto the base and taking leg by leg press each one onto the base. Add the cloven hoof detail with the knife point and add or refresh any other details to complete the model.

B. & M. Potterycrafts.

Thumb pot pig worksheet.

Clay.

Legs.   35grams. 8 cms

Snout.   15grams.

Ears.   12grams.

Body.   150 grams x 2.

Tail.   4grams.

Base.   100grams.

It is important to copy the worksheet to scale to ensure your model has the correct proportions.

64

Make a coil pot.

Clay coiling techniques.

B & M Potterycrafts.

65

B & M Potterycrafts.

Contents and Sequence.

Make a coil pot container. 67
    Make the coil pot base. 67
    Make and measure a coil. 67
    Form a hoop of clay. 68
    Attach the first coil to the base. 68
    Build the coil pot. 69
    Coil pot construction Worksheet. 70

Make a coil pot container.

Make the coil pot base.

Prepare the clay by rolling it into a ball, then squash it as shown in the picture, roughly into the size of the base which you need. Check the dimensions against the circle template. Try to ensure that the thickness is the same across the whole surface of the slab. If it is too thick in places it could cause the pot to slope. If it is too thin in parts the piece will be weak.

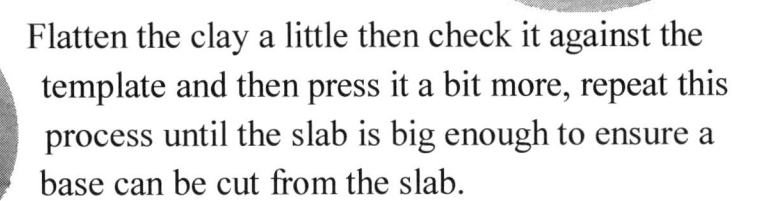

Flatten the clay a little then check it against the template and then press it a bit more, repeat this process until the slab is big enough to ensure a base can be cut from the slab.

Use the plastic knife to cut around the template, keep the knife upright and try not to cut under the template as the base will be thin in these areas.

Make and measure a coil.

The rolling technique begins by rolling the shape between the palms of the hands, making a short, fat sausage shape. It is important that the coil is kept to a uniform thickness along the length as it will be difficult to make a pot with coils which vary in thickness.

Having made the short fat sausage continue the rolling on the work surface, use the palms of both hands to roll the clay across the work surface and if the sausage shape is a long one splay the fingers to cover more area and control longer coils.

Complete a few rolls across the work surface, stop and check that the coil is of an even thickness. If the coil is thicker in some parts than in others the next rolling motion should apply pressure to the thicker parts.

The rolling and checking continues until you make the coil to the required length as measured against the template.

Form a hoop of clay.

The next step is to form the coil into a hoop of clay. Gently form the clay into an almost complete circle with the ends not quite touching. During the forming process don't force the clay or it will break, just apply gentle pressure with fingers and thumbs to encourage the clay to bend.

Dip your slip brush in the water and rub the water firmly into the end of the loop to form the slip which will bond the ends together.

Hold the ends between fingers and thumbs of both hands press the ends together with a slight sliding motion, one end against the other. Complete the joint by smoothing it with your finger.

Attach the first coil to the base.

With water and the slip brush create slip round the base where the coil is to be attached and also on the coil where it will touch the base. Firmly press the coil onto the base using pressure from fingers and thumbs.

Holding the coil in position on the base with the fingers and thumb of one hand press clay from the coil into the base with the tip of the thumb of the other hand. Gradually turn the pot round and press clay from coil to base until you return to the start point, the first coil is now firmly fixed to the base.

Build the coil pot.

Progressively make and add coils using the slip brush and water until you reach the depth of pot required. One point to remember is to place the joint of each coil in a different position on the pot because a line of joints will give a weak spot through the pot. Note that the joining of each coil to the lower one is also done as the pot grows as shown on the picture.

When you have made the pot to the depth required smooth the outside surface with fingers and thumbs to remove the worst blemishes and finish off the smoothing using the surface of the plastic knife flat against the pot like a spatula.

Stroke the smooth surface of the tools across the clay for the best results and try to start each stroke off the clay surface as the start of the stroke can mark the clay.

Note. The coils can be attached and smoothed inside as well as outside however if you just do the outside you can clearly see the assembly technique inside the pot.

B & M Potterycrafts.

Coil pot construction Worksheet.

Clay.

Base. 100 grams.

Coils. 35 grams each.

Templates.

Base. 7 cm

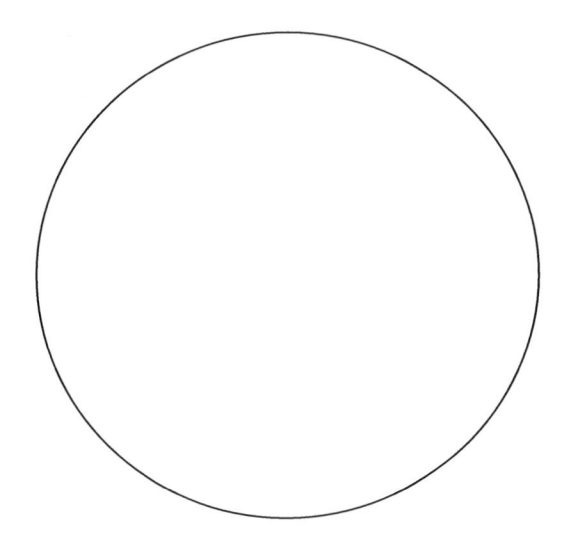

Coils. 19cms.

It is important to copy the worksheet to scale, use the dimensions shown to ensure your model is made to the correct proportions.

Pencil pot.

Slab pot techniques.

B & M Potterycrafts.

B & M Potterycrafts.

Contents and sequence.

Pencil Pot Container. 73
    Rolling the clay slabs. 73
    Cut out the parts. 74
    Prepare the cylinder. 75
    Crosshatch the edges. 75
    Make and apply slip. 75
    Join the edges. 76
    Add the base of the pot. 76
    Pencil Pot Worksheet. 78

Pencil Pot Container.

Rolling the clay slabs.

Start by rolling a piece of clay into a round smooth ball in the palms of your hands carefully removing any cracks or creases with finger pressure as they will become weak spots as soon as the clay is rolled and stretched.

When the clay is smooth it is patted flat before starting to use the rolling pin, you make it flat first because it is difficult to start the rolling process from the top of a ball. At this stage check again for any cracks appearing round the edges of the flattened ball due to stressing the clay by flattening it, if any appear repair them with pressure from your fingers. Repeat these checks and repairs throughout the process.

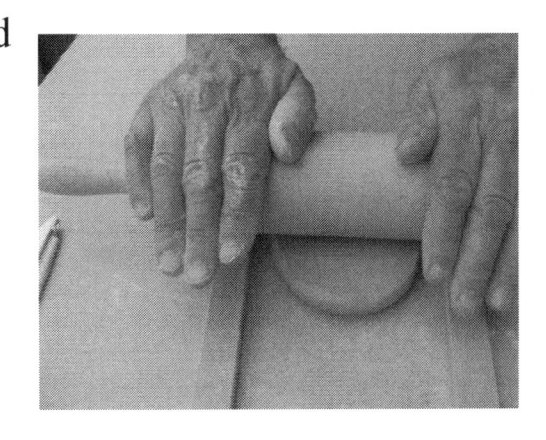

As you can see in the picture the hands are placed on top of the rolling pin not on the handles, this way you can exert more downward pressure through the clay to the work surface. Use of sticks of a set thickness allows you to produce slabs of clay to a known and uniform thickness every time simply by ensuring that the rolling only stops when the rolling pin is touching the top of both sticks.

Several times during the rolling it is advisable to peel and lift the clay from the work surface because it sticks to the surface and constant rolling won't make it thinner, lifting and replacing the clay on the work surface allows you to start again and makes the stretching of the clay easier. When the rolling is completed transfer the work to the smaller work surface.

Cut out the parts.

- Place the templates on the clay and cut out the rectangle and the circle. To ensure that the template doesn't move during the cutting process hold it in place with one hand while cutting with the other hand.

- Simply press through the clay and slide the blade along the work surface to ensure a clean cut, keeping the edge of the knife in contact with the template.

When making slab pot models it is important to keep the cutting edge vertical to the surface to be cut because if the knife is at an angle you will cut under one edge of the slab and over the other edge making it difficult to crosshatch and join cleanly to the next piece.

Try to cut in one clean motion, if you stop and restart you will probably leave a jagged edge.

Prepare the cylinder.

Place the rectangle on the work surface and hold it with one long edge touching the board.

Use fingers and thumbs of both hands to hold the piece upright whilst gently curling it round to form a cylinder with the edges to be joined not quite touching.

Crosshatch the edges.

Use the knife point to **crosshatch** both edges as shown in the picture.

Crosshatching is one of the keys to joining two pieces of clay. It consists of scoring the pieces in the areas to be joined. Use the point of the knife to mark clay.

Make and apply slip.

Next rub water along both edges using the brush, this creates **slip** which is needed to help bond the edges together.

The creation of **slip** is an important part of joining together two pieces of clay. The water from the brush is rubbed firmly into the clay surface until it turns light grey.

The slip acts as our glue helping us to bond the edges of the clay together.

Join the edges.
Join the two edges together using the following techniques.

Stand over the work and use thumbs and fingers to **press** the edges and bond them together, turn the work over and repeat this process on the other end of the cylinder. Ensure that the edges are firmly together from top to bottom.

The use of **pressure** is essential in successfully joining two pieces of clay when used in conjunction with crosshatching and slip

Finish off the jointing by smoothing the surface with fingers and finally the flat edge of the knife.

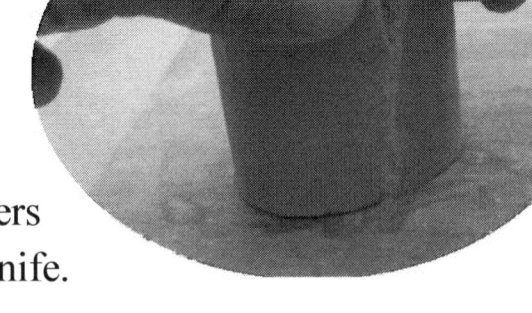

.

Add the base of the pot.
Place the cylinder on the circular base with an even spacing all round. Carefully draw a fine line around the pot to mark the base ready for crosshatching.

Remove the cylinder from the base and crosshatch just inside the fine line and around one end of the cylinder, the positioning is shown on the picture. The crosshatching on the base should be as wide as the cylinder is thick because this is the area to be joined.

Create slip on both crosshatched surfaces, turn the cylinder over and press it firmly onto the base.

Finally use fingers and the flat edge of the knife to clean up the joints.

If you wish to add designs to the pot you can mark the clay with a pointed stick or a pencil or cut out figures from thinly rolled clay to stick on the pot with slip.

B & M Potterycrafts.

Pencil Pot Worksheet.

Clay. 300 grams.

Templates.

Rectangle. 16.5cm x 7cm

Circle. 7cm diameter.

It is important to copy the worksheet to scale to ensure your model is made to the correct proportions.

Printed in Great Britain
by Amazon